I0116052

Supersedure

Xavier Hersom
Marti Steiner
Andi Hersom

Copyright © 2020
Xavier Hersom, Marti Steiner, Andi Hersom
Illustrated by Xavier Hersom
Photography Marti Steiner
Edited by Jessi Hersom and Pat Steiner

All rights reserved.
ISBN-13: 9780578699707 (Marti Steiner)

For all beekeepers...

Chapter One

It was the second text notification, but Dylan did not have time to stop and reply to Chris's message. The sun was already setting in the valley, trailing crimson light through the oak and maple trees that arched over the windy country road. The wind stung her scowling face and caused her short, purple and blue highlighted hair to fly wildly.

Dylan was perpetually late because she had to make do with her rusty bike. She did not have access to a car and would not until she could get a job and afford one herself. Since her father left, another car was not in the budget.

Dylan slid off the bike and let it crash onto the gravel driveway. She opened the mailbox and grabbed the mail. Rummaging through the adverts and bills, she stomped up to the plain, cookie-cutter house.

The dark walls of the dining room boasted photographs of Dylan, her sister, and two brothers—smiling kids frozen from a previous time. Images of ancestors and a favorite childhood dog lined the hallway. The likeness of a father figure was missing.

Mikie (her older brother) was sitting at the table with Zoe (her ten-year-old sister). Since he just graduated from college with a teaching degree, one of his many household responsibilities was to help with homework.

Dylan tossed the mail on the table.

"Hey Dylan, can you turn on the lights please?" Mikie asked without looking up from Zoe's paper.

Dylan sighed heavily and flipped the light switch as if it were a major chore. She pulled out her smartphone as she crossed the living room and slumped down on the worn corduroy couch.

Chris had texted: *What's up?*

Dylan gazed out the window.

Sometimes I wonder why I even try to be in a relationship, she thought. *It never works out in the end.*

Sighing, she looked back at her phone and texted: *Not much. Whatcha been up to?*

"Hey, how was your day?"

Dylan's mother sounded exhausted as she emerged from her office, rubbing her tired eyes. She sat down beside Dylan who ignored her.

"Fine."

Dylan's eyes were glued to her phone.

Her mother frowned. To her, it seemed like Dylan spent all of her free time on her phone.

"Dylan, why don't you go to scouts with Zoe tonight?"

Dylan glanced up with wide green eyes.

"No way! Why would I do *that!?"*

Her mother leaned closer to try to make eye contact.

"Listen, you can't just sit around the house all day. Maybe you should try something new... This morning I read a post about a young beekeeper's scholarship!" Dylan's mother smiled.

Dillan looked up from her phone with a stun-ed expression.

"What?"

"You get a free hive of bees!"

"Are you *crazy?"* Dylan laughed out loud. "I'm not doing *that!"*

"Well, we'll see. It's important you find *something* to do."

Dylan rolled her eyes.

"Whatever Mom..."

Dylan got up, stomped to the front door, and slammed it hard behind her.

What does she think I am, six? Why does she keep butting into my life? There is no way I'm doing scouts or some bee thing!

Cold air hit her red, hot face.

She took a deep breath and messaged her best friend Jamie: *I'm coming over.*

Dylan walked through the Moore's cool, damp basement. Jamie's older brother Trey was practicing his beat-up electric guitar.

"Hey!" Dylan shouted over the deafening music.

Trey nodded his head and grinned.

She walked into Jamie's dark bedroom. The walls were covered in band posters and clothes and trash cluttered the floor.

"What's up?" Jamie asked from her unmade bed.

Dylan dropped beside her and sighed.

"My mom has been getting on my nerves. She's at it *again!* This time she wants me to do some stupid *bee* thing!"

Jamie stopped scrolling through her phone.

"*Bee* thing?"

Jamie looked at Dylan as if she had three heads.

"You mean... like... save the bees kind of bee thing? Like *bugs?"*

Dylan nodded.

"Oh man, *that sucks*..."

Jamie's scarlet lips smiled as she tried to flatten

her messy, fire-red hair.

"I mean, I would be *so* pissed if I were you. Your mom is so weird, like, who in the hell wants to deal with *THAT?*"

Dylan's phone buzzed.

Chris: *Would you like to go to the game on Saturday? I have two tickets.*

Dylan: *I really wish I could, but I can't.*

She tried to think of an excuse which she had not used before. She was embarrassed to admit she had to babysit her younger brother and sister again.

"Who are *you* texting?" Jamie asked curiously.

"No one—"

Jamie grabbed the phone from her. *"Chris?* You're talking to *Chris?"* She slyly smiled.

Dylan blushed.

"We're just *friends.*"

"Yeah *right!"* Jamie tossed Dylan her phone back. *"Anyway,* we're thinking about having a party in a few weeks. Mom's gonna be in Vegas."

"Where?"

"Here! It'll be a *blast!* We're working on getting stuff for it now. Trey's band is playing."

"I'll see." Dylan sighed. "Sounds cool."

"Wanna bring *Chris?*" Jamie smirked.

"NO!" Dylan said, trying to keep a straight face.

At that moment, Jamie's mother swung open the upstairs door.

"TREY! TURN THAT CRAP OFF! I have a KILLER headache, and I have to be at the bar in TWO HOURS!"

Jamie groaned.

"You better go," she told Dylan.

"Ok... see ya later." Dylan grimaced then got up to head out.

Dave pulled his silver pickup into a parking space at the hospital and turned off the ignition. He sighed, slouched in his seat, and stared gloomily through the window. Ominous grey clouds crept above, obscuring the sun. He felt the same way—as if his life was overcome with darkness.

He reluctantly got out of the truck and walked into the building.

"Do you have an appointment Sir?" asked the young woman dressed in floral scrubs sitting behind the receptionist's desk.

"Yes Ma'am." Dave dryly smiled.

"Sign here"—she handed him a clipboard then nodded to the small waiting room— "and please

14

take a seat. The nurse will be with you shortly."
She smiled kindly.

"Thank you," Dave replied despondently.

He sat down beside a blond-haired boy with a cast on his leg.

"Does it hurt?" he asked, trying to keep his mind off things.

"Nope,"—the boy beamed at Dave then at his mother— "I'm getting it off today!"

"Well that's good news." Dave forced a smile. "How long have you had it on?"

"It seems like it's been *forever!* I broke it when I was playing soccer. But you know what, I still made that goal!"

"I bet you're excited to start playing again. It must have been awful not being able to do what you love."

"It was at first," the boy admitted, "but Mom started taking me to piano lessons instead. Now, I can play piano too."

"Phillip Roberts," the nurse called.

"That's me!" The boy stood up eagerly with his crutches.

"It was nice meeting you," Dave said.

"Nice meeting you too!"

The boy hopped his way toward the nurse with his mother following close behind.

Now the room was completely silent except for

a clock which announced the creeping passage of time. Beneath the clock was a cheap print of painted sunflowers. Dave noticed a poem engraved on a plaque under the print's frame, and he got up to read it. *Hopefully this is better than those old magazines,* He thought. He liked poetry.

Sunflower

Sprouts speedily
Birds scatter its seeds
Round brown face smiles seemingly
Unaffected by weeds
Thick green stem ever grows bold
Above other flowers like a tower
Stands proud, behold!
We should be like a sunflower
Its beauty always shows
Golden pedals bright
Never faces shadows
Only sees light

"Dave Mason."

Dave followed the nurse into the examination room. Deep down, he already knew what the doctor was going to say and what the results would show. It was time to face the facts.

As the nurse closed the door, he tried to keep his soul from being entirely clouded in darkness.

Chapter Two

While coasting down a hill, Dylan was admiring the flowering red bud trees when she rode her bike straight into a deep, water-filled pothole. While she avoided wrecking, mud sprayed up her back and all the way into her colorful hair. Dirty black water dripped off her helmet and in her face.

Great! My life completely sucks!

Dylan wiped the mud from her eyes with the sleeve of her jacket. She groaned as she rounded the corner of their driveway. Dylan unceremoniously deposited her bike in the ditch and gave it a hard kick—which gave her a stubbed toe.

Cursing under her breath, she limped to the mailbox and grabbed the assorted mail. She quickly shuffled through the damp envelopes.

"What is *THIS?*"

Her eyes caught onto a letter addressed to *Dylan Anderson* from the *Beekeeper's Association.*

She frowned and tore it open.

"Congratulations!" Dylan read through her teeth. She quickly scanned the paper. *"You have*

been awarded the young BEEKEEPER'S scholar-ship!" She paused, breathing heavily. *"We hope to see you on May fourth. We will assign you a mentor to help prepare you for installing your PACKAGE of BEES!* You have *GOT* to be KIDDING ME!"

Leaving the mailbox open, Dylan stormed up to the house.

She flung the door open.

"Zak how many times have I told you NOT to play with permanent markers!?" their mother yelled.

Dylan's seven-year-old brother Zak was running around the living room, dodging their mother who was in hot pursuit. She held a wet washcloth, ready to attempt to scrub his face clean. Finally, Zak jumped onto Mikie's lap and hugged him around the neck. Mikie laughed, realizing Zak had scribbled a brown beard on his face which resembled his own.

"MOM! WHAT IS THIS?" Dylan interrupted and waved the letter in front of her face.

She took the letter from Dylan and smiled as she read through it.

"Congratulations Dylan! Remember that beekeeping scholarship I told you about a few weeks ago? You won!"

Dylan ripped the paper out of her mother's

hands, crinkled it into a tight ball, and threw it across the room.

Mikie giggled quietly and looked mildly surprised.

"I'M NOT GOING!" Dylan shouted, shaking like a volcano about to erupt.

"*Yes,* you will!" her mom said firmly. "Dylan, it's time you get out and do something with your life!"

Dylan's eyes narrowed.

"*WHATEVER* MOM!"

She stomped to her room, slammed the door as hard as possible, and locked it. She flung herself on her bed and whipped out her phone.

Dylan: *Guess what!*

Jamie: *What?*

Dylan: *Mom actually got me that bee scholarship!*

Jamie: *WTH!*

Dylan wanted to reply but she was too angry to think.

There was a gentle knock.

"Come on out, let's talk," said her mother's

muffled voice from the other side of the door.

Yeah right. We already talked and I said I didn't want to do bees. Dylan thought.

"GO AWAY! I'M NOT TALKING TO YOU!"

"Give me a break." Her mother sighed. "I'm sure it's going to be a great experience. It won't be *that* bad."

Dylan groaned and pulled her white and green quilt up to her chin; she was done listening to her mother.

How can Mom think that messing with a bunch of stinging insects is good for me? There's no way she can make me go through with this!

As she slept that night, thousands of swarming bees chased her through her dreams.

Dave stopped his truck at the edge of his farm's field. He gazed miserably at his white hive—watching honeybees fly in and out of its entrance. He sighed heavily. After a few minutes, he started the truck and slowly drove home.

Chapter Three

Dylan glared out the passenger seat window of their old, beat up, gold minivan. She had only spoken to her mother that week when necessary, and since they were on their way to the bee meeting, she was definitely not going to start a conversation.

They pulled into the church parking lot, and Dillon got out and slammed the car door hard before waiting for her mother. Dylan groaned when she saw the paper sign taped to the from door of the church which read "Beekeepers Association Meeting this way" with an arrow pointing in the direction of the church hall.

The small room was crowded with a variety of conversing people, but most of them appeared over the age of sixty. Dylan immediately felt out of place.

It feels like I'm in a nursing home.

"Hello!" said a smiling man with white hair and large glasses. He shook Dylan's hand. "My name's Bob and I'm the president of our bee club.

21

Welcome! And your name is?"

"Dylan."

"Oh, my goodness!" Bob chuckled. *"You're* Dylan Anderson! We all thought *Dylan* was a boy!"

Dylan glared at her mother and whispered, "nice."

Her mother ignored her.

"I'll pick you up around eight."

Before Dylan could protest, her mother was out the door.

Dylan looked back at Bob.

"Go ahead and take a seat, we'll get started in just a few minutes."

All the tables and chairs were occupied except one—of course it was in the very front where she did not want to be—right next to a lady with long gray hair who was wearing a colorful tie-dye T-shirt, a flowing skirt, and Birkenstocks.

She looks way too excited to be wasting her life at this horrible meeting.

Dylan made her way to the open seat and sat down; careful not to make eye contact with anyone. She took out her phone and immediately texted Jamie.

Dylan: *Help me!*

"Hi there!" the overly happy woman said with

an enthusiasm that startled Dylan. "Are *you* the new scholarship winner?"

"Uh... yeah."

"Well, *congratulations!*"

The woman vigorously shook the hand Dylan was not texting with.

Dylan smirked. She found it perplexing that someone could be so enthusiastic about something this stupid. She had to refrain from laughing out loud.

What a weirdo!

"How EXCITING! It's great to see young people interested in bees!"

Dylan cleared her throat.

"*Thanks,*" she replied flatly.

"Alright, if everyone's ready, let's get this meeting started." Bob waited for the conversations to die down before he continued. "For starters, I'd like to ask our newest scholarship winner, *Dylan Anderson,* to please stand."

Mortified, Dylan slowly stood up; her face flushed as the room rang with loud applause and cheers.

This is the most embarrassing thing that has ever happened to me. Can this get any worse?

Bob nodded to her and she quickly took her seat.

"Now, we need someone who will be willing to

mentor this lovely young lady. Are there any volunteers?"

For a while, no one raised their hand.

If no one wants to be my mentor, then maybe I won't be able to keep bees after all! Dylan hoped.

Then the man behind her raised his hand.

Crap!

Bob quickly looked around. "*Uhhh...* would anyone *else* like the job?"

The room was still; no one volunteered except the man sitting behind Dylan.

"Ok then, Dave Mason will be Dylan's mentor."

While Bob started discussing the specifics of an upcoming state bee meeting, Dylan peeked behind to catch a glimpse of her new mentor.

The man seemed middle-aged. He had brown hair and sky-blue eyes *and* a ridiculous smile as he waved at her.

Dylan turned back quickly, rolling her eyes.

While everyone else paid close attention to what Bob was discussing, Dylan checked her texts from Jamie.

Jamie: *Who's at the meeting?*

Dylan: *I feel like I'm in the geriatric ward for*

insane beekeepers!

Jamie: *LOL*

After a while, the man sitting to her right slowly leaned close and whispered, "You know, you'll get more out of this if you put that phone away."

Well that's great, she thought with a scowl.

"Trust me—what Bob says is worth listening to." The man smiled.

Dylan shoved her phone in her pocket and folded her arms. She focused her attention on the worn, hardwood floor.

I can't believe Mom is making me go to these STUPID meetings! Not only do I have to learn how to keep BEES, there's no one here remotely close to my age!

Suddenly, Bob clapped his hands (startling Dylan who had mentally dozed off).

"Well that concludes the meeting tonight. Don't forget the honey festival is August tenth in Shepherdstown. I'll see you all next month when we'll discuss the growth you should be seeing in your hives."

People began getting up.

Thank God!

Dylan stiffly stood up, stretched, and yawned.

Her new mentor immediately came around the

table to greet her.

"Hello, I'm Dave Mason, and I'll be teaching you the basics of beekeeping!" He shook her hand.

"Hi, I'm Dylan." She briefly glancing at him then whipped out her phone to text her mother.

Dylan: *Where are you!? It's over. You're late!*

"It's nice to meet you! Hmm... let's see... does ten, Saturday morning work to set up your hive in my apiary?"

Dylan looked up from her phone with a confused expression.

"What's an *apiary?*"

Dave laughed.

"An apiary is a bee yard. It's where you keep your hives."

He pulled out a pen and paper from his jean pocket and wrote something down.

"Here's the address."

He handed her the paper.

Out of the corner of her eye, Dylan saw her mom wave from beside the exit door.

"Ok. I've gotta go," she muttered, then turned to leave with her mother.

"See you Saturday!" Dave called.

Bob walked through the crowd.

"Dave," he said in a concerned voice, putting a firm hand on his shoulder, "are you *sure* you're up for this?"

"Yeah, I'm pretty sure." Dave grinned to his old friend. "I think I can handle it."

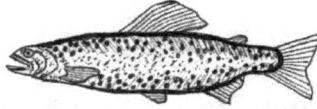

Chapter Four

Trey's music was so loud Dylan could physically feel the sound vibrate inside her chest.

"Hey Trey!" she yelled.

Trey continued to bang his shaggy black hair while shredding on his guitar. He did not hear her or even notice that she walked in.

Dylan did not feel the urge to scream to get his attention, so she just went into Jamie's room.

"Hey!" Jamie shouted from her bed, trying to be heard over the deafening music.

Dylan sat beside her and leaned back against the wall.

"Trey and a few other bands are playing at a party I'm having this Saturday. You need to start coming to these things again!"

Dylan frowned. She remembered how she felt out of place at the last party. There was too much smoke and beer. *I want to hang out with Jamie but how can I get out of going this party?*

The music stopped and Trey came in.

"Hey Dylan, want a drink?" He held up a bottle of neon yellow soda.

28

Dylan nodded.

He filled a red plastic cup and handed it to her. "Thanks."

Trey slid into the torn, upholstered chair that was too low to the ground for him.

I know! I'll use this beekeeping thing as an excuse.

Dylan turned to Jamie who was engrossed in her phone.

"I can't," she said, trying to sound convincing, "I have to go to the *bee farm* Saturday."

Both Trey and Jamie immediately stopped what they were doing and stared at her.

"Really Dylan! What the hell!" Jamie snapped. "You can't talk your mom out of it? Or fake the flu or something? Come on, you've got to at least *try!"*

Dylan sighed.

"Alright... I'll *try."*

Mikie's voice suddenly emitted from Dylan's phone. "It's your brother, PICK UP THE PHONE! It's your brother, PICK UP THE PHONE!"

It was a specialized ringtone she did not know she had. She had no doubt that Mikie had hacked her phone and created this as payback for never answering his phone calls when she was late.

Trey and Jamie laughed.

Dylan groaned and answered her phone

before it could ring again.

"WHAT do you *want?*"

"WHERE HAVE YOU BEEN? GET YOUR ASS HOME!" Mikie's muffled voice yelled.

Dylan held the phone away from her ear.

"We've been waiting an *hour* for you to come home so we can eat!"

"Alright!" She yelled back and hung up before he was finished.

Dylan rolled her eyes.

"I gotta go."

"Remember to get out of that bee crap and come to the party!" Jamie sighed. *"Bye."*

An important tradition for Dylan's family was that they always ate dinner together, ALWAYS. This was inconvenient for everyone, but their mother insisted.

Dylan shuffled in to find her family sitting around their dining room table; each plate filled with fish-sticks, Brussel sprouts, corn, and green beans.

"WHAT TOOK YOU *SO* LONG!?" Zoe scowled.

Dylan shook her head and sat in the empty seat beside Zak.

"Dylan," their mother said in an exasperated tone, "why don't you lead us in prayer?"

Dylan sighed as they all held hands and bowed their heads.

"Dear God," Dylan mumbled, "please bless this food we are about to receive. Amen."

"*Amen,*" everyone else said in unison.

They began eating their cold food.

"So," their mother said, waving around her fork, "how was everyone's day?"

Dylan stared at her plate, wishing she could look at her phone, but that was not allowed during dinner.

"I lost a tooth today!" Zak said with a smile, revealing a hole where his front tooth had been.

"*Awesome!*" Mikie said.

"You know what *that* means," Zoe said with enthusiasm, "it's *Tooth Fairy* time!"

Mikie wiped his bushy beard with a napkin. "Well, today while one of my students was dissecting a fish, he hit its spinal column and it jumped two feet in the air!" He gestured to show how high the fish jumped. "When I tried to catch it, I accidentally threw the scalpel I was using straight up to the ceiling! I probably almost got fired today." He chuckled.

Their mother laughed. Zoe was utterly impressed.

"*Eww,*" Dylan said with a look of disgust. "Don't talk about that when we're eating *fish sticks!*"

Mikie leaned down and whispered something in Zak's ear. Zak's eyes got wide with excitement and he looked across the table with a smile.

"Hey Zoe... do you like *seafood?*"

Zoe was picking at her fish stick with her fork. She scrunched up her nose. "Not *really.*"

With a mischievous grin, Zak seized the ketchup bottle and squirted it into Mikie's mouth. Then Mikie showed the contents of his red, chewed up food to Zoe.

"Get it!" Zak giggled. *"See food!"*

"Ewww! THAT'S DISGUSTING!" Zoe said, trying not to gag.

"Mom, do we *really* have to put up with this while we're eating?" Dylan said, aggravated.

"Mikie!" their mother said, trying to suppress a grin.

Mikie and Zak laughed and high-fived.

When their laughter died down, their mother cleared her throat.

"Look guys," she said seriously, "the last week of July I will be gone for training. So of course, I'm leaving *you* in charge." She nodded to Mikie.

Mikie raised his eyebrows and looked up from his food with a frown.

"What?"

"Give me a break, it's not that long."

Mikie grumbled.

Their mom turned to Dylan who folded her arms and looked down.

Their mom sighed.

"I hope you will learn as much as you can about your bees. Dave is really going out of his way to teach you... it's such a great opportunity." She smiled.

"Whatever Mom," Dylan said under her breath.

"Hey Dylan," Zak said, poking her arm.

She shot him a frown. *"What!?"*

"*See* food!" He laughed. On que, he and Mikie showcased their chewed-up food one last time and howled with laughter.

Chapter Five

Dylan was nervous.

She stared out the passenger seat window, hoping Chris would text back soon to keep her mind off what was about to happen.

Mikie was driving her to the place she had been dreading to go for the past week: Dave's apiary. Not only was she going to spend the evening with some strange middle-aged guy, they were going to 'install her package of bees'—whatever that meant.

Dylan's phone buzzed.

Chris: *I hope everything goes alright for you today.*

Dylan grinned.

Mikie glanced at Dylan out of the corner of his eye.

"Who are *you* texting?"

"No one," Dylan said under her breath while texting '*thanks*' back to Chris.

Mikie's eyes widened.

34

"So... are you messing around with that boy?"
"What?"

Dylan slowly realizing what Mikie was asking her.

"NO WAY! We're just friends!"

Mikie raised an eyebrow.

"Just *friends* you say?" he asked skeptically, scanning Dylan's face for the truth. "I guess I believe you. Well, you better not mess around, 'cause *I am* watching you!" He laughed.

Dylan slouched in her seat. "Oh my God! You are *so* embarrassing!"

The rutted gravel road crunched under the worn tires of the van. They drove beside a wide field of spring, bright green grass dotted with yellow dandelions.

"We're *here!"* Mikie said with a smirk; trying to annoy Dylan. But she paid no attention to him.

Her eyes were fixed on Dave's hive as he worked in it. Thousands of honeybees buzzed around his veiled face.

He looked down and pulled out a frame bursting with agitated bees as if it were nothing more than a slice of toast out of a toaster.

The van rolled to a stop, but Dylan did not get out.

Dave waved a yellow gloved hand at them, slid the frame of bees back in the box, and put the lid on his hive. As Dave walked slowly toward the van, the bees gradually left him and flew back to the apiary.

"Have fun *playing* with *bees!*" Mikie snickered.

Dylan shot a nasty glare at him then grabbed the bee suit at her feet, jumped out of the van, and slammed the door.

Mikie turned off the ignition and reclined in his seat. He chuckled to himself as he slid his green ballcap over his eyes—shielding them from the sunlight so he could doze off.

Dylan was hesitant to come closer to Dave; keeping an eye on his hive to make sure the bees would not suddenly dodge bomb her.

Dylan's phone buzzed, stopping her dead in her tracks.

Jamie: *You're coming to the party tonight right?*

"So, are you ready?" Dave asked enthusiastically, approaching Dylan.

She glanced at him briefly, then back at her phone.

"*Ready... for what?*" she asked while texting Jamie: *I can't I'm doing bees today.*

"Well,"—Dave paused to see if Dylan would look up at him; when she did not, he continued—

"today we're going to install the package of bees in your hive."

Dylan's eyes snapped up from her phone.

"What do you mean by that?"

"See that box of bees over by your hive?" Dave pointed to a small screened-in wooden box filled with honeybees clumped together. "They've gotta get in your hive somehow." He said excitedly.

Dylan stared at Dave and decided that he must be the craziest of *all* beekeepers.

"You mean I have to *dump* angry *bees* in a box?"

"Not just any old box, your new hive!"

Dylan gazed past Dave who was wearing a ridiculous grin and shifted her eyes between the box jam-packed with bees and the bright white hive resting next to Dave's worn hive. Then she looked back at her phone.

Dave signed to himself, becoming irritated in Dylan's apparent lack of interest.

Jamie: *Get the hell out of there and come to the party!"*

"Alright," Dave said, losing his smile, "go get your bee suit on and we'll get started."

She groaned to herself because there was no way out of the situation. This was going to happen.

The bulky, canvas fabric made her feel like an astronaut getting ready to explore a new world full of venomous aliens. She slipped the white, baggy pants over her jeans, then struggled to zip her wide, hooded veil attached to the bee jacket.

Disgruntled, she dropped her hands at her sides—giving up.

"Look," she said harshly to Dave, "I don't really want to do this. My mom made me sign up. I'm sorry. You can have my hive, I don't really care."

Dave was shocked.

"Why don't you want to keep bees?" He asked while adjusting her veil. "Beekeeping is the entire world in one small box. You've been given a gift that can totally change your life!" He smiled.

Dylan rolled her eyes.

"Come on, let's go!" he added reassuringly.

Dylan reluctantly followed Dave to her empty hive beneath the large budding oak tree. The closer she got to the package of bees the louder they sounded until it became a roaring buzz. A wave of fear shot through her and she whipped out her phone.

Jamie texted but it was impossible for Dylan to reply once her thick leather gloves were on (which she was not about to take off), so she dropped her phone in the deep pocket of her bee suit.

"Alright!" Dave said with giddy enthusiasm. "Ready to start?"

Dylan looked down at the box beside her stuffed with agitated bees.

"Not really," she whispered. Her heart was racing. She took in a deep breath to try to calm her frantic nerves. She felt nauseous and began to sweat.

"It's ok," Dave said, facing Dylan from the opposite side of her hive, "everyone's nervous the first time they install a package of bees. Don't worry, the bees aren't gonna bug ya!" He chuckled.

Dylan grimaced at the joke.

"We'll just take this one step at a time. Go ahead and pick up the package of bees."

Dylan's arms were shaking as she gingerly picked up the package—being careful not to touch the screen bees were frantically crawling on (which she was sure they could sting through). She promptly passed the package to Dave who used a yellow hooked metal tool to pry off a think piece of wood from the top.

"Now see that feeder can? I'm going to pull it out, and when I do, you grab the yellow strap that's attached to the queen cage."

Dylan blinked; it was as if Dave was speaking a

foreign. Language.

"Here we go! On the count of three... one... two..."

I don't want to be here; this guy is crazy!

".... three..."

Dave lifted the can and Dylan quickly removed the queen cage, but several honeybees escaped through the hole before Dave replaced the can. Dylan tried to dodge them as they bounced off her veil.

"Relax," Dave said coolly, "they can't hurt you with your suit on. Just stay calm and they'll settle down."

With forced effort, she refrained from veering about, and the bees eventually stopped flying around her face.

"Very good! *See...* that wasn't so bad."

Dylan said nothing, but deep down, she was starting to feel a little more confident.

"Now, take the cork out of the candy end of the queen cage, then put it between two of these empty frames."

Dylan glanced at the tiny box she was holding and saw the elongated queen honeybee

"So... why does the queen get her own box?" Dylan asked. "Why does she have to be separate?"

"She's a new queen who is a stranger to the drone and worker bees; most people are wary of strangers, and bees are the same way. The candy plug at the end of her cage will separate her until the workers eat through it and let her out. By that time, they will be used to her pheromones and accept her as queen. If she dies, the colony will also die, unless they can get a new queen."

"How *can* they get a new queen?"

"You can buy a new queen, the workers can build swarm cells that will produce queens, or they can make a supersedure cell."

Dylan felt as if everything Dave said went in one ear and out the other.

She held the queen cage firmly between two frames as Dave stapled it.

"This will keep her cage from falling to the bottom of the hive," he told Dylan. "Alright, now just remove the feeder can from the package and set the box gently on its side in the hive."

Dylan looked down at the bee box uncertainly.

"It's not as bad as you think it'll be."

Closing her eyes for a moment and holding her breath, Dylan quickly took the silver can out of the package of bees. She tilted the hole away from her as she slowly set it sideways on top of the frames in the hive. At first, the bee's wings sounded like heavy rain, then they became more frantic and their hum became as loud as a jet. Dave handed her the lid, and she carefully placed it on top of the hive.

"Wow Dylan, you did a really great job today!" Dave beamed proudly. "I think all of them made it in!"

Dylan was genuinely amazed she did it without being traumatized.

"Thanks."

"You'll see, in three days, they'll get to know each other, and they'll teach you all sorts of amazing things!"

"Yeah, ok."

"Alright!" Dave said, shaking her gloved hand. "We'll meet back here on Tuesday. Then we can make sure the queen was let out and inspect the hive. See ya then!"

Dylan walked toward the driveway.

She took off her hot bee jacket, got in the van, and slammed the door hard. Mikie woke with a jerk.

"So, how was it?" He yawned and stretched.

Dylan rolled her eyes.

"Whatever Mikie!"

She groaned and shoved her bee suit under her feet.

Mikie started the van and it made an ear-splitting squeal as they drove away.

Dave walked into his living room and hung his suit neatly on a coat rack. He then placed his hive tools and gloves in a handmade wooden box resting on a small side table.

Dylan threw her wrinkled suit and gloves in the corner of her room.

Dave sat in his favorite easy chair. He looked up and his sky-blue eyes shined as he grinned from ear to ear.

Dylan laid on her bed and glared at the ceiling. Her phone buzzed and she rolled over on her stomach and grabbed it from the nightstand.

Jamie: *WHERE ARE YOU? Trey's band is playing now!!!*

Dylan did not reply.

A few uneventful days later, Dylan was back in the Moore's basement.

"So, *why* haven't you answered any of my texts

and why didn't you come to the party?" Jamie asked sharply.

Dylan sighed.

"I've just been too busy lately. You know, I have to go back to Dave's farm today. I can only hang out a few minutes."

Jamie stopped scrolling through messages on her phone.

"Why didn't you *listen* to me? You should have told Dave you didn't want to do bees!"

"I DID!"

"You should have just *left.*"

"I couldn't..."

"Why not?"

Dylan got silent and looked away.

"I don't know."

She would never admit it, but Dave seemed like a nice guy who was obviously excited to teach her something new. She would have felt a little bad disappointing him.

"Whatever!" Jamie said, aggravated. "In six weeks, mom's gunna be gone again and we're planning the biggest party we've *ever had!"*

Dylan hesitated. She knew that Jamie would not let it go if she missed another party. *This is the same time my mom will be gone,* Dylan thought, *but how the heck am I going to get past Mikie— he's always watching—uhgg.*

Dylan groaned.

"I'll see, Mikie won't let me go if he finds out because the cops showed up last time. I'll try my best."

Jamie shook her head and began painting her long fingernails black.

"You should *go,*" Jamie said, rolling her eyes, "you have to go to the *bee farm* soon."

"Alright," Dylan scowled, "see you later."

Chapter Six

Dylan held two heavy frames full of honey and agitated bees as Dave used his hooked hive tool to pry apart another. Her aching arms were beginning to fall asleep and she was burning up in her bee suit.

"I HATE this!" Dylan muttered quietly under her breath.

"How many more are there?" she whined. Dave's hive was overflowing with frantic bees and it was difficult to tell which frames had enough honey to harvest.

"Just one more," Dave said, pulling it out and examining both sides. "You have to wait until the bees completely cap the honeycomb—otherwise there will be too much moisture in the honey, and it will ferment. "

"Wait—so you're telling me that if we take un-capped honey, we end up with jars of *beer?"*

Dave chuckled.

"Not exactly, but some day you can make a honey wine called mead."

Dylan's eyes lit up.

"Are we going to learn how to make mead in bee school today?"

"No."

Dave pulled an additional frame from the box and Dylan moaned.

"But do you know about the Telling of the Bees?"

I DON'T want another long lesson about bees right now! Dylan thought. *I'm hot and tired, and I'm ready to go home!*

"In Europe, beekeepers would tell their bees about special occasions in their lives like births, weddings, reunions, and deaths. If a beekeeper forgot to share these important life events, the bees would impose a penalty such as swarming, not producing honey, or dying."

"That's a little weird." Dylan said.

"Remember, you should always talk to your bees about what's going on in your life."

Dylan raised a raised an eyebrow; sweat dripping off of her face.

"*Ok.* Thanks for the history lesson. Are we done here? I'm dying."

Dave used his yellow bee brush to gently brush the bees from the honey frame back into the open hive. Dylan scowled as he handed her the last heavy frame so he could close the hive with the lid.

"Here, I'll take some of those from you," Dave said with a smile, stepping around to her.

Suddenly, he jumped back and bolted away from the hive.

"Hey! Where are you going?" Dylan hollered as Dave tore through the grass to his truck.

He came to a stop and began slapping his lower legs where his boots met his pants.

"GOD BLESS AMERICA!" Dave shouted, trying to verbally restrain himself. He flailed around, doing some sort of crazy dance.

Dylan could not help but laugh out loud.

After a while, Dave settled down, leaned against his truck, and began taking off his suit. Dylan came up to him and put the frames in the truck's bed.

"What happened?" she asked, hiding her smile.

Dave groaned.

"I didn't tuck my pants into my boots all the way."

He looked down past his shorts at his bare legs. They had many red, puffy welts on them. He sighed.

"Let this be a lesson on making sure your suit is secure. Especially when taking the bee's honey!"

"I definitely will." Dylan lost her smile, feeling a little guilty for laughing because it looked very painful.

"Listen, I'm probably going to have a hard time driving. Do you have your license?"

"Yeah, I just got my permit last week."

"Would you mind driving me to my house? I need to take some anti-allergy meds. Then we can work on extracting the honey."

"Sure," Dylan said, feeling a little nervous, "but I'm not the best driver."

"Can you drive a stick shift?"

"Uhhh... no."

"Well then, fasten your seatbelt, because you're gonna learn today!" Dave chuckled, then grimaced as he eased himself into the passenger seat.

Dylan walked slowly to the driver's side and got in.

How difficult can it really be? she thought. *I know how to drive the van.*

"You ready?" Dave asked with a grin.

"Yeah, I guess so," Dylan said while buckling herself.

"Alright then." Dave uneasily shifted in his seat. "The trick is to step on the clutch, then when it's time to start moving, slowly let out the clutch while you give it some gas. Go ahead and put in the clutch and start the truck."

Dylan pushed the clutch to the floor and turned on the ignition.

Piece of cake, Dylan thought.

"Ok, put it in first gear and let's go!"

Dylan let the clutch out and pushed the gas pedal down.

The truck lurched a few feet and stalled.

"Oh no! Sorry…"

Dylan looked at Dave who was trying to get his legs in a comfortable position.

"That's ok, let's try again."

Her heart now pounding, Dylan slowly put the clutch to the floor and started the truck. She made sure it was in first gear, and this time, gave it more gas as she let her foot off the clutch. The truck jerked even more violently and immediately stalled.

"Crap!" She said, feeling discouraged.

"Hey, you can't learn if you don't try. Just go again."

This time, Dylan noticed Dave had a white knuckled grip on the handlebar by the door.

"Are you sure?" Dylan asked.

"I know you can do it!" he said reassuringly.

She took a deep breath, and once again, turned the key in the ignition. This time she eased both pedals, and while the truck started with a slight jerk, it kept moving.

"Great!" Dave beamed proudly. "Just keep it in first gear and don't drive too fast—my house is just at the end of the field." Dave relaxed his grip on the handle.

Dylan grinned to herself.

"As you get to the driveway, step on the clutch just before you hit the brake," Dave said as his house came into view.

Dylan accidentally stepped on the brake pedal instead of the clutch and the car came to a screeching halt and stalled. She was so embarrassed, she could not look at Dave and felt on the verge of tears.

Dave laughed it off. "You know what, that really wasn't too bad for your first time driving a stick-shift. I'm sure you'll *beecome* better with practice."

Relieved he was not mad at her, Dylan chuckled. They got out and walked up a few steps to his porch. One side of the porch had a few stacked hive boxes, and the other had something which resembled a metal trash can with legs and a crank handle.

"Just wait here a minute and I'll be right back."

Dave slowly made his way into the house, looking like a cowboy who had ridden a burro for a hundred miles.

Dylan took off her bee suit and sat on the shaded porch steps. The cool breeze felt great through her short, sweaty blue hair.

Yeah... this is exactly how I want to spend my Saturday. How much longer will this take? Dylan thought.

Dave hobbled back through the door. In his arms, he held some empty jars and two bottles of water.

"Let's extract this honey so you have an entry for the honey show."

Dylan sighed tiredly.

"Look, I don't need to be part of that. Don't you want to go sit down or something? I can call Mikie to pick me up early."

"I *am* going to sit down," Dave said, passing her an ice-cold water. "*You* are the one who will be doing the extracting."

Dylan frowned. She gratefully took the water, twisted off the plastic cap, and downed the whole bottle.

"*Ok*," she said, taking a deep breath, "let's get this over with."

"Grab a frame of honey and uncap it with this knife." He handed Dylan a long thin knife and nodded at the trash can looking thing on the porch. "Just cut off the cappings on both sides and place the frame in one of the baskets in the extractor."

"What?" Asked Dylan. She did not entirely understand what Dave meant and did not want to mess something up again like when she drove his truck.

"I'll do one side for you so you can see how it's done. It's really very simple."

He took one of the frames and showed her how to carefully cut only the very top layer of the wax. "The goal is to leave the cells intact so the bees can reuse them; it takes about seven pounds of honey for the bees to produce one pound of wax, so it's best to let them recycle it as much as possible."

Dylan sighed, wishing Dave would just hurry up.

See... wax on, wax off!" he said chuckling to himself; flipping the frame to show the side that was still sealed in wax and the uncapped side, oozing with honey. He handed it to Dylan so she could finish the job and he slowly sunk into a nearby rocking chair.

It took a while for Dylan to get the hang of maneuvering the knife across the frames without crushing the wax cells, but it was not long before she had an uncapped frame in each of the extractor's baskets.

She sighed with exasperation; not only was she exhausted and hot, now her hands were sticky too. She could not wait to get home to take a nice long shower and go straight to bed.

"Now all you have to do is spin it." Dave pointed to the bent handle on the top. "The centrifugal force will cause the honey to fling out of the frames and drip down to the bottom of the extractor. Then we can bottle it."

Rolling her eyes, Dylan unenthusiastically began spinning the machine.

She quickly become fascinated by how the honey strung out of the frames, which spun so rapidly that they became a blur. However, it did not take long for her arm to grow tired, then cramp.

As if holding those heavy frames wasn't bad enough. My arm is KILLING me!

Dave came around and looked down in the extractor.

"Good job Dylan!" He smiled. "The frames are almost emptied on that side."

"On *that* side?" Dylan looked at Dave, aghast.

"Yeah, once you finish spinning the frames out on one side, you have to flip them around and spin them on the other."

As she was flipping the frames around, Dylan asked: "Are you feeling better yet?"

"Yeah, my legs are throbbing still, but they don't burn anymore."

"How are your arms?" Dylan half grinned.

Dave laughed.

"Once you're done with these frames, I'll put the rest in my freezer, and we'll finish another time.

Once Dylan finished, she sat on the porch steps again, waiting for Mikie to pick her up. She shook out her aching arm.

Dave glanced at her, while he was cleaning out the extractor.

"Don't worry," he said with a grin, "beekeeping is always the most work in the spring. In the summer, you'll only have to feed your bees and make sure the hive is strong going into the fall. When winter rolls around, you kick your feet up, and enjoy your honey!"

"Great—only six more months," Dylan said under her breath.

They could hear the distant sound of the van making its way up the long driveway.

"We're done for today, tomorrow we will filter and bottle your show honey. Here, before you go, try this piece of come honey from your hive."

Dave handed Dylan a spoonful of waxy light honey.

"Do I eat the wax *too?*"

"Sure, it won't hurt you."

It was as if the gates of heaven had opened up; it was the best honey Dylan had ever tasted. *Maybe this work will be worth it after all.*

Supersedure

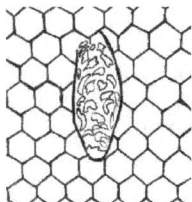

Chapter Seven

The apiary was alive under the cloudless blue sky. Thousands of honeybees worked a sea of white clover flowers; the sacks on their legs heavy with orange pollen. Dylan was watching this action from the passenger window when Mikie said: "Hey, I might be a little late picking you up. I gotta take Zoe to scouts."

"Can you *try* not to be late? It's going to be a hot day."

Dylan glanced at Chris's text.

"I shouldn't *beeee* too long." He laughed loudly, totally pleased with his own joke.

Dylan groaned and rolled her eyes.

She put her suit on in the long grass then walked up to Dave who was already working in his hive.

"Hello Dylan! How've you been?" Dave waved a gloved hand which was covered in bees.

"Ok, *I guess*," Dylan answered sulkily.

"By the way," Dave said, taking out a frame full

of jittering bees, "did you know there are tons of famous beekeepers?"

"Really?" Dylan asked in disbelief, stepping back as bees began flying off his frame.

"Oh yeah! Aristotle, Ben Franklin, Thomas Jefferson, Martha Stewart, Morgan Freeman, and most importantly: Sherlock Holmes." He grinned.

"Wait... Sherlock Holmes isn't even a real person!"

Dave ignored Dylan's comment as his eyes focused on the center of the frame he was holding.

"Hey, come look at what's going on here."

Dylan cautiously went to the other side of the hive next to him.

That looks really weird, she thought.

Underneath the fidgeting bees was a long, peanut-shaped wax cell; much larger than any of the worker or drone cells.

"What's *that?"*

Dave turned his veiled head toward her, then back at the frame.

"It's a supersedure cell. This means the queen isn't laying enough or is failing in some way."

"What! That's bad!" Dylan said, looking concerned. "If you lose your queen, you lose your hive!"

"Not necessarily *lose* my hive, but change is

going to happen."

"Can't you just rip that supersedure thingy out? Maybe the queen will get better in a few days." Dylan frowned.

Dave carefully put the frame back in the hive and looked at her with a smile. "Life doesn't stay the same. Supersedure is important for the health of the hive. The queen has done her job and now it's time for a new queen to take over. The new queen is going to emerge in a few days, and soon, she will be ready for her royal duties. The hive will be renewed." Dave grinned as he looked at Dylan's upset expression. "It'll *beee* an awesome adventure!"

"Seriously!" Dylan snapped. "I don't know how you can joke about this... all of that time *wasted!*"

"Wasted? How so?" Dave looked at her inquisitively. "The new queen has comb, pollen, and honey in place. The world has been handed to her... all she has to do is make something of it!"

Dave accidently knocked the hive tool off the corner of the hive beside Dylan. As she bent down to pick it up for him, she heard something tear and she immediately stood up. *Oh my God!* she thought frantically. *This is NOT good!*

"I RIPPED my pants!"

Dave's head shot up. "Quick, get away, or you'll get stung!"

As Dylan tor through the field, she suddenly felt liquid fire on her right leg.

"SHIT!"

When she arrived at the driveway, she made sure there were not bees following her, then quickly whipped off her suit. Above her right knee was a swelling red welt.

Crap.

"Did you get stung?" Dave yelled from the hive. "Make sure the stinger's out!"

The pain had faded a bit from fire to hot and Dylan did not see a stinger.

Dave watched as he capped his hive and went a few feet away from it—waiting for the bees to retreat. A few minutes later, he approached her.

"Hey, are you ok?"

"Yeah... one got me on the knee."

"Well, congratulations," he said, patting her on the back, "you're now an official beekeeper. Welcome to the club!"

"Great." Dylan said, wincing.

"Welp, I guess we're done for today. I have an extra suit you can borrow until you get yours fixed."

"But... my brother isn't supposed to pick me up for half an hour!"

Dave paused in thought. "Hmm... do you wanna go get ice cream? My treat!"

"Ok... I'll let Mikie know."

She took out her phone and called her brother.

Classical music enveloped Dave's truck as they drove to the ice cream stand.

"Is it alright if I change the station?" Dylan asked.

"Nope. Sorry, I only listen to classical music while I'm driving," Dave said, turning the steering wheel. "It helps me focus."

Dylan sighed and looked out the passenger window.

"What type of music do you listen to?" Dave asked.

"Classic rock, alternative, electronica. Stuff like that," she said flatly.

"Classical is where it's at!" Dave smiled.

Dylan snickered and looked at him with raised eyebrows. "How can you like *classical* music? It's *SO* boring."

"It's not boring," he assured her, "it's exciting! All the instruments in an orchestra play their part—the harmony and melody work together in rhythm—otherwise, the song would die. Kinda like how honeybees work together in a hive."

"Ok," Dylan grinned. "If you say so."

Supersedure

Dave pulled into the ice cream stand's parking lot.

They sat down at an outdoor picnic table surrounded by dandelions.

"See anything wrong with these flowers?" Dave asked before eating a spoonful of mint ice cream.

Dylan inspected the ordinary, yellow flowers. "Not really," she said while softening her hard, chocolate ice cream with her red, plastic spoon.

"There are no honeybees anywhere around here and dandelions are a great source of pollen. It used to be, when I was a kid, you would find honeybees everywhere. But now, you don't see them unless you're close to a hive. Because of mites, pesticides, and diseases, almost all honeybees HAVE TO have beekeepers take care of them. Once in a while, you'll hear of a successful feral hive in the woods someplace, but now, almost all honeybees can't survive on their own."

Dylan swallowed.

"I didn't know that! "

"It's sad. That's why our job is so important. Did you know that one-third of our produce is pollinated by bees?"

"Wow," Dylan said with wide eyes.

She watched as a warm breeze caused the dandelions to sway in gentle waves.

"Anyway," Dave said, "so tell me about yourself. What are some of your hobbies?"

Dylan sighed. "Actually, I don't have any."

"*Really?* Huh, so you must have a lot of friends then?"

She looked down.

"Well... I *used to* anyway, but now I basically just have one friend. But I don't really think it really matters."

"What makes you think friends don't matter?" Dave asked with a concerned expression.

"Well, having a bunch of friends in high school is a big scene. To be *that* kid, I would have to pretend I'm a clone. You know, wear the same clothes as everyone else, listen to the same music, all that crap. I ditched that plan when I finished my junior year."

"Interesting—well to that, I have to say: it's important to *BEEE* yourself!" He laughed.

"That's not even funny." Dylan rolled her eyes but could not help but laugh at how lame the joke was.

Mikie pulled up and honked the van's horn.

"I'll see you later Dylan," Dave said as she stood up. "Have a good week!"

"You too." Dylan smiled. "Thanks for the ice cream!"

Dave sat in his easy chair and threw his keys on a small table beside it (which was cluttered with mail, a framed photograph, and an out-of-date answering machine with a blinking red light).

He signed and pressed the 'play' button on the machine.

"You have one new message," said the electronic voice.

"Happy Birthday..." a man's voice said sarcastically. "This is a courtesy call... Mom would've wanted it." The message ended.

Dave's eyes shifted to the photograph—it was a picture of him and his brother Rick. They were smiling and Rick's arm was thrown over his shoulder.

Dave rubbed his aching forehead and sighed.

Chapter Eight

It was the night of Jamie's party.

Dylan carried Zak to his bedroom, laid him on his bed, and firmly tucked his soft blue blanket around him.

He rolled over on his side.

"Can you read me a story?" he asked as she tried to leave the room (she was preparing to sneak off to the party).

"I can't now... I'm tired." She forced a false yawn.

"Please," he whined.

"Dylan, read Zak a story!" Mikie's voice yelled from the living room.

She groaned. "What do you want me to read?"

"This one!" he said, handing her a blue book with a smiling frog on the front.

"I'll read from where I left off," Dylan said as she removed the bookmark.

"Ok," Zak said smiling. He wrapped his blanket more snuggly around himself.

Dylan sat beside him and cleared her throat.

"Rana cried. 'If there is anything you can do to make me a frog again, I would be forever grateful.' 'Well, there is not much I can do, except...' the fairy child said with twinkling eyes and a smile, 'there is one thing. If you have learned that you are wonderful as you are, and we all have gifts that make us special... then... and only then... can the spell be reversed.'"

Dylan stopped as she heard Zak snoring.

A cool breeze blew in from his half-opened window.

Aha! This is how I can get out unseen! Dylan thought with a grin.

The James Bond theme song played in her head as she slowly raised the window and quietly stepped out. She did not dare to take her bike from the front porch because Mikie would see her and know he would know she was up to something.

Thunder rumbled in the distance as she began jogging along the dark road.

The rain stung her face by the time she got halfway to the Moore's house.

Damn it! I should have brought a raincoat or something! she thought. *I don't even have a flashlight.*

She took out her phone and used the light from it to see the road. Finally, after what seemed like an eternity, she made it to Jamie's house.

Dylan opened the basement door. Blaring electric guitar and bass shook the house, strobe lights flickered, and smoke hovered above the floor. Kids were crowded around Trey and his band, their fists pounding in the air to the beat. Some of them had painted faces that glowed in the black lights and everyone was drinking.

Jamie emerged from the center of the crowd.

"HEY!" she yelled, waving a beer in her hand. "WHAT TOOK YOU SO LONG? THEY'VE BEEN PLAYING FOR THIRTY MINUTES!"

"IT WAS DARK," Dylan shouted angrily, "AND I HAD TO WALK... AND..."

Jamie ignored Dylan and turned back to the band.

"Never mind." Dylan sighed.

A tall boy with long hair and a band shirt came up to Dylan. "Wanna beer?" he asked, holding one in front of her.

"Thanks," Dylan said unenthusiastically, taking it from him.

He left to join his friends.

Dylan stood awkwardly alone for some time, then walked up to the crowd. The music was so loud it started giving her a headache.

I don't even like this music anyway, she thought, looking around at the screaming crowd. Jamie was the loudest of them all—her hair looked like a wildfire as she repeatedly banged her head.

What am I doing here? Jamie doesn't want to hang out with me.

The party was so loud, Dylan was worried it would wake the rest of the neighborhood. She set her untouched beer on a table covered with food wrappers, maneuvered her way to the exit, and stepped outside in the wet grass.

The thunder collided with the booming music as sheets of rain poured from the sky.

Well that's just great!

She leaned against the house under the eaves to keep dry. Dylan knew she would have to get a ride home.

Mikie is going to kill me!

She took out her phone and dialed his number.

"Come on Mikie... *pick up!"* she whispered into her phone which continued to ring. She called three times, but he never answered.

"Great!" She groaned, looking at her phone screen. "It's almost midnight! *Now* what do I do?"

She scrolled through her contacts and found Dave's number. Sighing, she rubbed her blood-shot eyes and called him.

What do I say? What will HE say? What will he think of me now?

"Hello?" Dave sounded startled.

"Hey, I'm sorry, I know it's late, but I was wondering if you could give me a ride."

"Yes! Where are you? Are you in trouble?"

"Not really," Dylan said remorsefully. "I'm at Sixty-Two Setting Sun... I'm sorry."

"No problem! Stay put, I'll be right there."

She shivered and slumped against the peeling block wall.

I can't believe how stupid I am! This sucks.

Soon, headlights lit up the Moore's driveway. Dylan ran through the rain, got into Dave's truck, and quickly shut the door behind her. She slouched in the seat. The rain, windshield wipers, and soft classical music were the only sounds.

"Are you ok?" Dave asked, looking at her seriously.

"I tried to call Mikie," she sighed, "but he didn't answer."

"Are you *ok* though?"

Dylan glanced at Dave who looked concerned. It was nice to know someone truly cared about her.

"I'm fine." She smiled. "Thanks."

They drove in silence. After a few miles, Dylan

said, "Ok, you can drop me off here."

Dave stopped his truck next to her mailbox and she hopped out.

"Listen," he said seriously, "if you are ever in any kind of trouble, you can always call me—ok?"

"Thanks," Dylan said with a tired smile, "I really appreciate it."

"See you tomorrow at the honey festival!"

Dave waved then drove slowly away.

As Dylan laid exhausted in her warm bed, she saw red and blue lights flash through her window as sirens shrieked toward the Moore's residence.

Supersedure

Chapter Nine

Dylan walked sluggishly out of her bedroom and into the sunlit living room. Her bloodshot eyes squinted at the blinding yellow morning light.

Mikie stared at her from the couch.

"GOOD MORNING SUNSHINE!" he said annoyingly. "How was *your* night?"

She glared at him and opened her mouth.

"Save it, sit down!" he snapped, pointing to the cushion beside him.

Dylan sat and crossed her arms.

Crap. Here it comes...

"So," Mikie began, "did you go to a party last night?"

Dylan smirked.

"Do you think I would be *up* this early if I went to a party?"

Mikie's eyes narrowed, scanning Dylan's face for the truth.

"Hmm... I guess I could believe *that."*

Thank God, he fell for it! Dylan thought with relief.

"Oh, by the way," she sneered, "you have to be ready to take me to Dave's in fifteen minutes, 'cause we're *goin'* to the bee festival!"

"Dylan! You could have told me earlier so I had more time! I didn't plan on going anywhere this morning!"

He got up, shook his head, and threw his phone at her.

Dylan smirked; pleased with herself.

Today might be a good day after all.

The festival was loud and crowded. A rainbow of tents covered tables laden with bee paraphernalia. In the colorful shade, people sold everything bee related: from honey, beekeeping gear, salt and pepper shakers and honey pots, to fancy hives artistically painted with different farm scenes. Dylan recognized some of the people as members of the bee club.

She followed Dave to a large white tent where dozens of honey jars were displayed on a table.

"Hello! Welcome to the honey festival!"

Dylan recognized the hippy bee lady who had congratulated her at the first bee meeting.

"Please fill out this registration form."

She slid a clipboard to Dylan and Dylan carefully handed the woman her jar of honey.

"See those guys over there?" Dave whispered to Dylan, nodding toward two beekeepers chatting at the end of the honey display. Dylan looked up from the clipboard and peered at them. One had a long red beard and the other had silver hair. Both were carefully inspecting the jars of honey.

"Yeah?"

"They always win. I'm not asking you to enter because I want you to win—I want you to try even when the odds are against you. Always give it your best shot."

Dylan signed her name at the bottom of the form.

"I've heard that *so* many times. Do you know how many people say that?"

"Yes, and I mean it."

Dylan handed the woman the clipboard then turned back to Dave.

"Hey, I heard there's free food for participants, and I'm starving!" he said.

"What are they serving?" Dylan asked skeptically.

"Pulled pork!"

"Ewww!" Dylan gave a look of disgust. "You can have mine."

"Great!" Dave grinned. "Let's go!"

Live bluegrass music filled the air as they made

their way through the crowd.

"Where did all these people come from?" Dylan asked, impressed with the volume of bee fanatics.

"We're lucky because we live in an area with a lot of backyard beekeepers. In many places, there aren't hardly any."

"Oh."

After each had ordered pulled pork and a dessert, they found a spot to sit under the shade of an ancient maple tree.

"So, tell me about your family," Dave said, swapping Dylan's pulled pork sandwich for his honey bun.

"Well, you've met Mikie, he's a huge pain in the butt, but he does help the family a lot. When he's not bossing me around, he's actually pretty cool to hang out with. I have a younger sister named Zoe—she's not too bad for her age. And there's Zak, who's pretty much how you'd image any seven-year-old boy to be. Mom's a pretty good mom I guess—when she's not signing me up to work with thousands of stinging insects!" Dylan grinned.

Dave laughed.

Dylan got silent, leaned back, and sighed.

"Dad left just before Zak was born—

apparently, he thought he'd be better off with a woman a little older than Mikie. We haven't heard from him since."

Dave frowned.

"Well, I never had kids myself, but I would say it's his loss. He sure is missing out."

"Thanks... So... What about your family?"

Dave wiped his mouth with his napkin and got up.

"Hey, let's go check out that bluegrass band! They sound like they'll *beee* pretty good."

Dylan groaned.

"*Please* stop with the bee puns!"

"Ok." Dave grinned. "*Well, maybeee.*"

A few weeks later, the wildflowers began to die, and the dearth season began. Mikie drove Dylan to the grocery store to buy sugar so she could make syrup to feed her bees. As they rounded the corner of the baking isle, she noticed Trey checking out with two cases of beer.

They did not acknowledge each other.

Chapter Ten

Dave was so weak from the chemotherapy, he could not get up from his easy chair; his whole body felt like lead.

Great, he thought miserably, *and today is the day Dylan and I are supposed to check our bees.*

With a trembling hand, he picked up the phone and dialed her number.

"Hey Dylan... how are you doing?" he said in a rough voice. "Good... I was wondering, do you think you could check my bees for me? I'm not feeling very well... Ok, thank you."

Putting the phone back on its stand felt like lifting a ton of bricks.

His tired eyes closed as he fell into an exhausted, deep sleep.

Dylan knocked hard on the door and woke Dave with a start.

"Come in!" he called.

She opened the door and stepped inside. The cluttered walls were filled with scenic photographs, paintings, and a framed certificate. Her eyes stopped when she saw Dave slouched in his chair.

She walked around and sat on the leather couch beside him.

"Your bees are looking a lot better!" she said proudly. "I'd say in a week there'll *beee* enough new workers to making a split." She joked.

He slowly turned his head to her and smiled.

Dylan lost her grin.

He looks awful, she thought.

"Good! How are *your* bees doing?" he asked in a raspy voice.

"There's a lot more drawn out comb than before," she said, checking out the inside his house.

Dave groaned to himself.

Dylan turned to scrutinize him more closely.

"Uh... do I need to wash my hands or wear a mask or something?" she asked, half-joking.

Dave paused.

"No, It's nothing like that."

Dylan scanned the room and noticed the photograph on the side table.

"Is that one of your beekeeper friends?" she asked, pointing to the picture.

"No," Dave said meekly, "that's my brother."

"I didn't know you had a brother!"

"Well... we don't talk much anymore." Dave

sighed, leaned back, and closed his eyes. "I'm really tired, you can help yourself to a snack in the fridge. I'm just going to rest here a while."

"Ok, thanks. I hope you feel better soon."

While on the way to the kitchen, Dylan paused to look at the photographs on the wall. She discovered the framed certificate was an honorable discharge from the Army.

"Hey, I didn't know you were in the military," Dylan said, turning to Dave. But he had already fallen asleep.

Dylan carefully took the blanket from the back of the couch and laid it over him. Then she quietly headed to the kitchen. She opened the fridge, grabbed a bottle of water, and immediately downed half of it. While catching her breath, her eyes fell on a stack of opened mail on the otherwise pristine counter. The top letter was a bill from the hospital.

Well, at least he got checked out by a doctor, she thought.

After polishing off the rest of her drink, she flipped to the next letter which was a water bill. Then she saw a letter from Hospice.

What?

Glancing up, she made sure Dave was still sleeping, then quietly slid the letter out of its open envelope.

Mr. Mason
Thank you for enquiring about Hospice. Hospice
provides expert medical care to keep patients
comfortable—

Suddenly, Dave moaned and shifted. Dylan quickly shoved the letter into its envelope and slipped it back in the pile.

She silently made her way to the door and gently shut it behind herself.

Mikie frowned as he stared down at the engine of the gold van. Out of the corner of his eye, he saw Dylan exit the house and make her way toward him. He groaned.

Great, now what? He wondered.

She walked up and leaned against the van.

"Let's do something fun. Take me to the movies!"

"No, if you can't *see*—I'm a little *busy* right now."

"Come on," she whined, *"I'm bored."*

Mikie slammed the hood shut and turned to Dylan.

"Look, I would *love* to, but I can't. I'm just praying this thing will last me another year... sorry squirt. Let's go inside and play cards instead." He grinned.

Dylan sighed as they walked up to the house.

Chapter Eleven

Dylan had not seen Dave for a week, and when Mikie dropped her off at his farm to check her bees, Dave did not show up.

That's strange, Dylan thought. *I'll just do his bees for him again. I wonder if he's still sick?*

The blinding sun beat down on her as she pulled out each sticky frame from his hive.

I wish they could make these suits a little cooler. It feels like I'm in a sauna.

She looked at the bottom of a full frame of brood and nurse bees and found what was left of the supersedure cell which Dave's new queen had emerged from. Already the new queen was laying thousands of tiny rice-shaped eggs in the perfect hexagonal cells.

Well, things definitely ended up working out in this hive, Dylan thought as she replaced the hot metal lid. *I can't wait to tell Dave how good this looks!*

Dave was awake in his chair but overwhelmed with exhaustion. He glanced at the picture of his brother and he reached shakily for the phone, but paused, then dropped his arm to his side.

At that moment, Dylan knocked on the door.

"Come on in!" Dave said in a frail voice.

She walked through the dimly lit room and took a seat beside him. Her eyes wide as she stared. Dave had dark circles around his watery blue eyes and was unnaturally pale.

"Hey, what's going on with you?" Dylan asked seriously. "Have you been to the doctor?"

Dave cleared his scratchy throat.

"Yes."

Dylan leaned closer to him.

"*And?* What did they say?"

Dave's bloodshot eyes shifted to the floor; he could not bear to look at Dylan.

"A lot," he said quietly, "and... nothing really..."

Dylan's heart sank and she felt physically ill. Suddenly, it all made sense. *Oh my God, the hospice letter was for him!*

Dylan felt as if someone had punched her in the stomach—she could barely breathe. She stood up, got within inches of his face, and looked straight into his eyes.

Her expression twisted in anguish.

"WHY... DIDN'T... YOU TELL ME!"

Dave did not look up.

With tears filling her eyes, Dylan stormed out of his house and slammed the door as hard as she could.

Dylan ran.

She did not care where she went, she just wanted far away. Her aching heart pounded hard in her chest, but she could not stop. The trees lining the neighborhood were nothing but a blur.

She flung their front door open and raced to her bedroom.

"Hey, what is wrong with you!?" Mikie asked and tried to grab her as she ran by. She shoved him as hard as she could, bolted to her room, and slammed the door.

Dylan gripped the sides of her dresser; her arms violently shaking. Hot tears streamed down her face. Breathing hard, she screamed, and in one swift motion, she flung everything from the top of her dresser to the wall.

Her vase shattered in a thousand pieces.

Mikie rushed in the room and grabbed her by the arms.

"Dylan! What happened?"

Dylan could not answer, she only sobbed in Mikie's crushing hug.

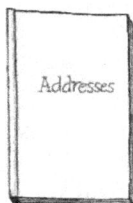

Chapter Twelve

Dylan was laying on her bed with her arm resting over her eyes—shielding them from the sunlight which peeked through her drawn window blinds. She felt that the word was nothing but dark and miserable.

Her phone buzzed.

She remained motionless until the incessant buzzing annoyed her to the point that she wanted to throw her phone out the window. Then she groaned and finally sat up to check the many messages.

Jamie: *Why haven't you been answering!?*

Dylan sighed, not wanting to deal with her.

Dylan: *Dave is really sick.*

Jamie: *So what? Who cares! You need to come to Trey's party on Saturday.*

Dylan: *I care! And the cops showed up last time.*

Jamie: *Really! It was no big deal. There was a fight, some kids got taken away, and they made us end the party.*

Dylan: *I'm not going.*

Jamie: *LOSER.*

A week had passed, but time no longer had meaning to Dylan. She spent most of it lying on her bed and staring despondently at the colorless ceiling. Her head ached and her puffy eyes throbbed. She felt like she had cried every tear she would ever own and there was nothing left of her but an empty shell.

I can't believe he didn't say anything. How could he do this to me?

She heard a sharp knock and Mikie stepped into her room. She did not bother to turn and look at him.

He came to the side of her bed and slammed his hands hard on the mattress, causing her to jump.

"Listen! I know you're upset, but you need to

get off your sorry ass and quit being such a selfish bitch!"

Dylan's red eyes met Mikie's which were wide and serious—an expression quite uncommon for him.

"Dave is the best friend you've ever had. You NEED to make up with him. GO NOW!" He pointed to her open door, then promptly left.

She curled in a fetal positon and stared at the blue wall.

He's right... I have to go.

After a while, she picked up her phone and slowly dialed Dave's number.

"Hi... this is Dylan," she said, trying to sound happy. "Would it be alright if I came over today? Ok, see ya soon."

She got up, looked through the mirror above her bare dresser, and tried to smooth out her tangled blue and purple hair. The dark circles around her eyes looked nowhere near as bad as Dave's had. Dylan could not forget the last disturbing image of him. She was afraid to discover what he might look like now.

"Mikie's right," she muttered to herself. "I've been a total jerk! Dave must feel like crap after the way I treated him... and *he* is the one who's sick."

85

Dylan slipped on her tennis shoes, tied them tightly, then grabbed her phone from the bed and shoved it deep in her jean pocket.

Feeling hopeful, she quickly left the house.

Heat shimmered off the pavement. She strained her eyes from the blinding, hot sun; after staying in her dark room for over a week, she felt like a nocturnal animal.

Dylan grabbed her bike from beside the mailbox. It had rained several times the past few days and now it showed major signs of rust and squeaked as she rode it, but she did not care.

The warm summer breeze swept through her hair as she traveled down the winding road. She felt free as if released from an emotional prison. Inhaling deeply, she smelled the sweet honeysuckles that lined the edge of the road.

Dylan would have smiled if she had not been so full of fear.

Dylan paused outside Dave's house.

Although she could not wait to see him, she also dreaded what was behind the front door.

I wonder how many more times I'll be able see him? I hope I don't say anything stupid.

Dylan hesitantly knocked.

"Come on in!" Dave's voice sounded stronger than it had before.

Dylan slowly stepped in and saw Dave sitting at the head of the dining room table, looking up from a book. He smiled affectionately.

A wave of relief washed over Dylan and she smiled back.

"Hey Dylan! Come have a seat."

Dylan shut the door, crossed the foyer, and sat down beside him.

He was not as pale as he had been the last time and looked like he was doing somewhat better.

"I owe you an apology," he said, looking at her straight in the eyes. "It's been hard for me to process what's going on, and I definitely realize it was extremely unfair of me not to tell you. I'm truly sorry, and I hope someday you will be able to forgive me."

"It's ok, I was *beeeing* a jerk."

They both laughed.

"You a jerk? Never! You were just upset, and I can understand that. So, what've you been up to?"

Dylan sighed.

"Not much," she said, looking around the room. She eyed the book laying open on the table.

"What are you reading?"

"Poetry," Dave said, clearing his throat.

Supersedure

"Upon delicate petals
Of amethyst clover flowers
You collect nectar and pollen
Passing away busy hours
To towering white palace, you fly
You are its protector
Surrounding sisters
Share in golden treasure
And merrily the hive hums
In a song, old and sweet
Until a robber breaks within
A battle you must defeat!
With venomous dagger, you stab
Through black tangled fur
But your mind clouds
As earth becomes a blur
In sacrificing your life, you saved
The Queen; heart of the hive
Whom repopulates the colony
Again, her kingdom will thrive"

Dylan beamed. *"Of course* it would be about bees."

"No doubt!"

"Far out."

"Good one!" Dave chuckled.

Dylan smiled and sighed. "So how have *you* been?"

"I've been feeling much better, but you know, I've missed our goofy conversations."

"I've missed them too."

"Wanna play cards?" Dave asked with a grin.

"Sure!"

Classical music softly played from another room as Dave shuffled and dealt the cards.

"This song is actually ok," Dylan confessed.

Dave rearranged the cards in his hand.

"Coming from you, I will take that as the highest compliment." He smiled. "Your turn."

Dylan laid down a pair of matching cards then picked up another card from the deck.

As Dave took his turn, she saw the picture of him and his brother out of the corner of her eye.

"So, when *was* the last time you talked to your brother?"

Dave laid some cards on the table.

"We don't talk anymore."

"Why not? Did you get in a fight? I know what that's like. A couple weeks ago, I found Mikie's stash of chocolate and... well... you know. Boy, he was pissed!"

Dave picked up a new card and half-smiled.

"No, it's nothing like that. Sometimes I wish we could just start over."

"It's never too late to start over! You've got a

phone, just call him!"

Dave stared off and sighed.

"No... I can't... I don't want to bother him about this." He looked at Dylan straight in the eyes. "Learn from my mistake."

"Ok," she said, shifting in her chair and shuffling the cards. Dave was looking depressed, so Dylan decided to change the subject. "You know, I've been wondering, *why did* you start keeping bees?"

Dave looked up from his cards with a passionate smile.

"There's a peaceful order to them. All the bees rely on each other during every aspect of their lives. When something threatens the colony, each worker will risk its life to protect the hive. To see how simple it is for the bees to coexist and work together, it gives me hope that there might be more to the human race than killing each other and bringing disharmony to our world. Really, we could learn a lot from them."

"Yeah, I guess that's true."

"And if that's too deep for ya, they give me honey and nothing relaxes me more than opening the hive and hearing that buzzing roar. I bet most people who don't keep bees would find that totally unbelievable!"

"I'm pretty sure you're right about that!" Dylan

laughed.

She looked back down at her cards and smirked; when it was her turn, she laid them all down.

"I won!"

"You sure did!" Dave said with a tired smirk. He leaned back in his seat and rubbed his swollen eyes. Dylan could tell he was growing exhausted.

Time to go, she thought.

Dylan sighed. "Well... I should probably get going now, Mom will have dinner ready soon. But thanks for having me over. It was really great to see you."

She stood up and gave Dave a huge hug.

Tears formed in her eyes, but she managed to hide them.

"Sure thing—you're welcome to come over anytime."

"Thanks."

They broke away and Dylan slowly headed toward the living room.

"Till next time," Dave said waving. "Don't worry, *beeee* happy!" He grinned. .

She laughed and waved back.

Dylan gripped the door handle, but before she left, she noticed Dave's address book laying on his side table. She made sure Dave was not watching her, then quickly shoved it in her pocket and slipped out the door.

Dylan jumped on her unmade bed. She opened the stolen address book and flipped through the thin pages until her finger hit the name *Rick Mason.* She took out her phone and dialed the number.

This has to be him.

She waited until a man's voice answered.

"Hello... is this Rick Mason? Hi. You don't know me, but I'm a friend of Dave's. Is he your brother? I just wanted to let you know...."

Dylan told Rick everything she knew the best she could, while forcing herself not to cry. Saying it out loud made everything more real and it hurt.

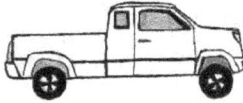

Chapter Thirteen

Although it was dusk and it would be dark soon, Dylan decided to stop by Dave's. Her bike squealed as she rounded the corner to his street, and she noticed two people were sitting on his front doorstep.

Hmmm... who could that be?

As she rode closer to the house, she realized it was Dave and the man from the picture. Both men were laughing, completely absorbed in their conversation.

Awesome! It's Rick!

Dylan beamed, knowing she had done the right thing by calling him.

Not wanting to interrupt them, Dylan continued on home. Dave noticed her as she passed, waved, and gave her a knowing nod as she rode by.

Dylan waved back and her heart sang.

Dylan was sitting at the table, working intently in a notebook.

Mikie looked over her shoulder.

"Hey, that's really good!"

"You weren't supposed to be looking!" Dylan blushed and tried to cover up the flowers she was drawing.

"Well, it's not *quite* as good as my stick figure people!" Mikie laughed.

Dylan's phone rang and she answered it immediately.

"Hello... are you sure you feel well enough? Alright!" she said enthusiastically. "I'll see you in a bit!"

"Was that *Dave?*"

"Yes... he said he wants to meet me at the apiary today. Can you give me a ride?"

"Your chauffer awaits," Mike said, rubbing Dylan's hair into a mess. He grabbed his keys from the table.

It was a beautiful day; the weather was cool for summer and the sky was endlessly blue. Dylan gazed out the passenger window and watched as the long golden grass swayed in the gentle breeze.

"Crap!" I forgot my phone at home!" Mikie sighed and shook his head. "Can I use yours? Mom was going to call to let me know what to pick up at the store."

Dylan groaned.

"I didn't bring mine."

Mikie pounded the steering wheel. "Damn it! Well, I'll have to drop you off and run home."

"No problem, we have to feed the bees and check for mites, so it'll be a while anyway."

They slowly pulled up to the apiary, but only saw the tree and both hives.

Dave was nowhere in sight.

Then, Dylan saw crumpled white in the grass.

"*Oh my God...*" She whispered.

It was as if everything was in slow motion. Mikie hit the brakes with a jerk and Dylan leaped out of the vehicle before it had come to a complete stop.

All she could hear was her heart beating.

"I'M GOING TO GET HELP!" Mikie screamed, spinning out of the driveway.

The world was a blur as she ran to where Dave lay.

It had been a week. The cicadas and crickets sang as Dylan zipped the veil of her bee suit closed and grabbed the handle of the bucket filled with sugar water. She walked over to Dave's hive and stopped beside it, her heart in her throat, staring at the lid. Suddenly she dropped the bucket, fell to her knees, and wept, hugging the hive.

She told the bees everything.

Dylan lay motionless on her bed; her red, swollen eyes barley able to keep open. She had not gotten much sleep because every time she closed her eyes, she could not erase the image of Dave's body laying alone in the field. It had been two weeks since his death, but she was just coming to terms with the loss. Every day, images of his suffering nagged at the back of her mind and she had to constantly replace them with all the good memories they shared together.

Someone knocked at the door.

Her mother walked into the room and sat down on the bed beside her.

"A woman came by today and talked about his will," she said sympathetically.

Dylan sighed.

"Of course, Dave wanted you to have his bees. *And...*"

She threw Dave's truck keys on the bed, patted Dylan's shoulder, and left.

Dylan sat up, grabbed the keys, and looked at them closely in the palm of her hand.

A huge smile spread across her face.

All the windows were rolled down and the music blared. Her colorful hair flew in the wind. She spun out of the driveway and yelled triumphantly.

She was free.

Finally, she parked in an empty cul-du-sac, reclined in her seat, and smiled. It was great to feel happy again.

Out of the corner of her eye, she noticed a folded envelop stuffed in the crevice of the seat.

Dylan was written on the front.

She carefully opened it and began to read the hand-written note.

Dylan,
Hey there. I need to let you know how special you are, because you changed my life.

Dylan stopped as her eyes filled with tears. She did not want to finish reading the letter because that would mean every single thing Dave wanted to tell her would have been said. By keeping the letter unread, Dylan though that it would be like keeping part of Dave alive.

But he would have wanted me to read it.

You have so much to offer the world. Go out there and live it to the fullest!

She smiled and dried her eyes so she could read again.

I know you will make this world a better place. Don't be afraid to try new things, and love everyone. You are a true friend, and that's a beeeutiful thing (sorry couldn't help myself).

Dylan laughed softly through her sobs.

Thank you for being my friend.

Dave

Epilogue

Dylan was almost done checking the bees when she saw the convertible pull up. A tall boy with blond hair stepped out of the car and waved.

Dylan waved back and slowly walked toward him, making sure the bees did not follow.

"Hey Chris! How've you been?" Dylan grinned.

"Good," he said in a low voice. "I wanted to say that I'm very sorry about what happened to your friend."

Dylan sighed. "Thanks..."

"And, I was wondering," he shifted nervously, "would you like to go out for ice cream?"

"Sure!" A wide smile lit up Dylan's face. "I have to do one more thing at the hive first. I'll be right back."

Dylan's boots swished through the yellow grass as she went up to Dave's old hive. She reached a gloved hand into her deep pocket and pulled out a jar of honey. Attached to it was a blue, first place ribbon from the honey festival.

"Thanks for everything," she whispered. Dylan placed the honey on the top of the hive. She straightened the ribbon, paused, and smiled. Then she turned and walked back to Chris.

"You ready?" He grinned as she got in the car. "Let's go!"

Dylan realized she was wrong when she thought that by reading Dave's letter, her memory of him would die. She would always share his gift of friendship and hear his laughter in hum of bees.

Supersedure

Supersedure

Supersedure

Supersedure

And that is a *beeautiful* thing.

Xavier Hersom is an award-winning orchestral composer, writer, photographer, and illustrator. Xavier was the director of photography for the movie *Supersedure* and wrote the film's music score. His other books include *Transition, Rana's Wish, Musings of an Appalachian Child*, and *Inheritance*. He is passionate about history, traveling, volunteerism, and beekeeping. He started beekeeping when he was sixteen after winning a young beekeeper's scholarship from his local bee club.

Marti Steiner directed the movie *Supersedure.* She is also the author of 'ker͵givər. Marti is a motivational speaker and is passionate about impowering people and communities to be their best. She is a life-long member of her state and local bee club. She believes honeybees are *beeautiful* and is an advocate for their preservation.

Andi Hersom played "Dylan Anderson" who was the lead character in the movie *Supersedure.* She has trained over 1,000 Recovery/Life Coaches. Andi enjoys connecting with others and spending time with family.

This book is based on the movie *Supersedure*.

www.SupersedureTheMovie.com

Like us on Facebook
Supersedure

www.ingramcontent.com/pod-product-compliance
Lightning Source LLC
Chambersburg PA
CBHW050537280326
41933CB00011B/1624